Puppies • Cachorros

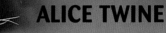

ALICE TWINE

TRADUCCIÓN AL ESPAÑOL:
José María Obregón

PowerKiDS press. & **Editorial Buenas Letras**™

New York

Published in 2008 by The Rosen Publishing Group, Inc.
29 East 21st Street, New York, NY 10010

First Edition

Editor: Amelie von Zumbusch
Book Design: Julio Gil
Photo Researcher: Nicole Pristash

Photo Credits: Cover, pp. 1, 5, 7, 9, 11, 13, 15, 17, 19, 21, 24 (top left, top right, bottom left, bottom right) Shutterstock.com; p. 23 © www.istockphoto.com/Eileen Hart.

Cataloging Data

Twine, Alice.
  Puppies–Cachorros / Alice Twine; traducción al español: José María Obregón. — 1st ed.
      p. cm. — (Baby animals–Animales bebé)
  ISBN-13: 978-1-4042-7687-1 (library binding)
  ISBN-10: 1-4042-7687-4 (library binding)
  1. Puppies—Infancy—Juvenile literature. 2. Spanish language materials I. Title.

Manufactured in the United States of America.

Websites: Due to the changing nature of Internet links, PowerKids Press and Editorial Buenas Letras have developed an online list of Web sites related to the subject of this book. This site is updated regularly. Please use this link to access the list: www.powerkidslinks.com/baby/pup/

Contents

Contenido

Baby dogs are called puppies.

A los perritos bebé se les llama cachorros.

4

A puppy has four legs, four paws, and a tail. Puppies wag their tail when they are happy.

Los cachorros tienen cuatro patas, cuatro garras y una cola. Los cachorros mueven la cola cuando están contentos.

6

Some puppies have pointed ears. Other puppies, like this one, have **floppy** ears.

Algunos cachorros tienen orejas puntiagudas. Otros cachorros, como éste, tienen orejas **suaves**.

8

There are many kinds, or breeds, of puppies. This puppy is a **border collie**.

Hay muchos tipos, o razas, de cachorros. Este es un cachorro de **pastor escocés**.

10

Labradors are one of the best-liked breeds of puppies.

Los **labradores** son una de las razas favoritas de cachorro.

12

Dalmation puppies are born with white fur. After a few weeks, their spots start to form.

Los cachorros de **dálmata** nacen con pelaje blanco. Después de unas semanas, les salen manchas negras.

14

Newborn puppies drink their mother's milk. As they grow older, puppies learn to eat out of a bowl.

Los cachorros recién nacidos beben leche de sus mamás. Al crecer, aprenden a comer en sus platos.

Puppies need lots of sleep. They sleep between 18 and 20 hours a day.

Los cachorros son muy dormilones. Los cachorros duermen entre 18 y 20 horas cada día.

Puppies love to play. They like to run, jump, and chase things. This puppy is playing with a ball.

Los cachorros también son muy juguetones. A los cachorros les gusta correr, saltar y perseguir muchas cosas. Este cachorro está jugando con una pelota.

20

Puppies make very good pets. They are friendly and fun to play with. Does anyone you know have a puppy?

Los cachorros son muy buenas mascotas. Los cachorros son muy amigables y juguetones. ¿Conoces a alguien que tenga un cachorro?

Words to Know • Palabras que debes saber

border collie / pastor escocés

dalmation / dálmata

floppy / suaves

labrador

Index

Índice